The Mercies
of Perry County

poems by

Juliet Hinton

Finishing Line Press
Georgetown, Kentucky

The Mercies of Perry County

ACKNOWLEDGMENTS

I am grateful to the following journals and presses where some of these
poems initially appeared:

"At the Broken Places" and "Almost Family" now titled "Unto Dust." *Cantos*
Link: https://www.mobap.edu/about-mbu/publications/cantos/
"Calvary Baptist Church, Spiritual Mother and Antique Pink Dress."
Delta Poetry Review Link: https://deltapoetryreview.com/?fbclid=
IwAR26eMmrOnAlFQsiQR18f3zTb9GxhbTMAog7XuaGNsb5WB7Z9
dNM6tdS0
"Childhood Baptism," "Graining God in the Morning Hayfield," and "Moses'
Arms." *Penwood Review*
"Memories Cruel Harvest" previously "The Last Cow Horn." *Valley Voices: A
Literary Review*
"What We Cannot See" *Cantos*
"Wedding Rings and Chicken Wire Dredging" *Tipton Poetry Journal*; Link:
https://issuu.com/tiptonpoetryjournal.

Publisher: Leah Huete de Maines
Editor: Christen Kincaid
Cover Art: Juliet Hinton
Author Photo: Juliet Hinton
Cover Design: Elizabeth Maines McCleavy

Order online: www.finishinglinepress.com
also available on amazon.com

Author inquiries and mail orders:
Finishing Line Press
PO Box 1626
Georgetown, Kentucky 40324
USA

Contents

Introduction

Highway 98 Recounts the Pain of Perry County 1

The Trees of Perry County 2

When the Cows Pastured in the Trees 3

Shangri-La Comes to New Augusta, Mississippi 4

Memories Cruel Harvest 5

The Antique Pink Dress 7

Wedding Rings and Chicken Wire Dredging 8

My Black Spiritual Mother 9

The Plowman's Tears 10

Calvary Baptist Church 11

The Baptism at Arlington 12

Serpent in the Red Dirt 13

The Meanest Man I Knew 15

Thirteen Bridges 16

Graining God in the Morning Hayfield 17

At All the Broken Places 18

Spilling Wisdom 19

What We Cannot See 20

A Smoke Filled Marriage 21

Cheating 22

Lighting One Post at a Time 23

An Elegy Written at the Old Bethany Graveyard 24

The Pain that Kept the Grandfather from Dying 25

Unto Dust 26

Author's Bio 29

To my angels in Perry County

Introduction

These twenty-four poems share my metaphoric reflection of the landscape of my home, Perry County, Mississippi, the topography of memory, and the thriving faith and strength of family. For nine generations now, my ancestors have lived in Perry County. I spent my childhood as a freckled faced tomboy who fed her cousin mud pie from an old wood stove, climbed, and clawed the curved terraces of corn with her yellow dog, Susie, and pulled catfish from the pond while yelling out across the field to the old house among the chinaberry trees and one-hundred-year-old oak. These poems, I believe, emerge from the feminine vision found in Southern letters from Welty, O'Connor, Alice Walker, and Ellen Gilchrist.

Highway 98 Recounts the Pain of Perry County

I run through Perry County like a river of tears.
My dotted lane lines that streak from Beaumont
to Richton, from New Augusta
to heartache telegraph centuries of secret;
my blacktop glazes with surprises and doubts.
I can see the past and the future on the other side.
So many days they look children all alike. The learning
lessons that sting.

The questions of the county travel on me hungering
for different destinations but I go only one way.
Perry County covers its curves with prickly pines
and moans.

Loggers ply asphalt as if they were scrolling
the triumphs of genes. Why not? The more
trees Perry County cuts down, the more space
there will be for howls. Bridges sway
across me in moonless nights
like mourners at Scottish wakes.
I parade across schools, down streams

to churches, hospices that fill beds with residents
who have lost their sense of history's hold on them.

The Sheriff arrested seven ghosts wandering
down my tarred pathways; they all confessed

they longed for the desire to be loved.
They just did not know how to find it. I was not
going to help them multiply the county's misery.

The Trees of Perry County

An oak planted a hundred years ago by our grandfather welcomes the morning doves even as red ants invade its roots and travel through its deep crevices. The ghosts of the forests that we have invaded and cut down escape in the winter wind to burn their memory into our thoughts. They have become a part of us, and we have of them. Fireplaces are their crematoria of dreams and ours as well. Generations of Hintons have been buried in their dead torsos. Their rings encircle the heads of our dead. But it is a transitory martyrdom; the wood decays slower than the bones of our lost. Trees will inherit the land even though they have been hauled away to Mobile or Atlanta. Their shadows lament lost love and hold grudges. So akin to the people who planted and lumberjacked and walked over forest graves confident that they have vanquished the trees. But these marred generations of narrowly spaced growth rings speak a voice you do not always want to hear. The trees refuse to silence them. Nor do these poems. What are poems, after all, but whitened leaves.

When the Cows Pastured in the Trees

The Leaf River was a part of us, and we were a part of it,
but not in a good way. It had the discourteous habit
of intruding into our houses and turning our land
into mud hole swimming pools, making the cows
scurry for pasture into the trees, their hooves hanging over
the limbs like twitching cane fishing poles.

In some ways, Perry County's elite citizens
were responsible. They shantied too damn close
to the Leaf's banks and thought the river would respect
the boundary between dry land and soggy river bottom.
But when the river got bloated and vomited all over
their houses and cars, they wondered why,
ignoring more than 200 years of bad history
with the Leaf. Or they built their houses on sand
and not on piers high enough to escape the Leaf River's wrath.

The muddy Leaf waters rushed through their rafters and gun racks.
 Some of the so-called smarter Perry County folks parked
their cars at the end of their property, next to
the nearest road, thinking escape was possible,
but they did not factor in the necessity of walking on water.

But perhaps the worst offender of river lore
was the onery fool who bought a piece of land
with a damn on it (to stop the Leaf from ravaging
crops and livestock) and then first thing tore
the damn down angering his neighbors down
river who depended on the dam to protect their lives.
The only response the dam breaker had was
"Twas my damn, damn it." He sure as hell ensured that.

3

Shangri-La Comes to New Augusta, Mississippi

At seven, my make-believe world
was the row of our cornfield.
In the field next to our pond,
I loved to watch the moon chase
the goblins and other critters away.
Then, my slender, little body longed
to turn into a string of corn silk
and slide between the kernels or float
on a breeze to our neighbor's field.

Memories Cruel Harvest

Down a splotchy, grass-lined dirt cow path,
just off Wingate Road, I remember riding
in my uncle's faded red Chevy, bouncing

across gopher-holed cow pastures
toward evening feeding time, the moon
peeking through rusty October clouds.

My uncle let me sit on his lap
and drive even as his callused
Delta Pine hands gripped mine
as we slowly passed fields
with faded corn

falling victim to the red clay
that sheared and lurked
under lime-streaked clods.

Leaning against his chest, I didn't see
the bone cancer harboring a grapefruit-sized
tumor ball inside him. Years later,

his two ribs, cut away, left a hole
in his chest slinking into his blood-brown liver,
his jaundiced eyes blearing across
the kudzu coiling terraces
where he once kicked up his yearling youth.

Now, these fields were filled with vines overtaking
any green that was once there.
Greedy maggots had gotten
them into patches of yellow squash shriveling them
into a blight.

The brim pond dam had turned hazy brown
as hay left in the soon-setting sun,
its mid-day fire consuming the fish.

At sunset, the black cow horn blew,
and I knew the land had felt his pain.

The Antique Pink Dress
New Augusta, MS, April 2005

In my antique pink, maid of honor dress,
I was a soup kettle mixture of emotions
as I assisted my friend slip
into the hoop skirt and underclothes,
her ruffled skirt over it as her beaded blouse slipped
over her pounding heart.
Last of all I placed her mother's veil
on her head.

Our emotions were high, the harder she cried,
the harder I prayed the ceremony would be over soon.
The happiest day of her life drug on
as a funeral procession of her dreams.
On the first day of her marriage,
she would have clearer vision
of what true love did not consist.

She was wooed by a lover
but ended up wed to a bickering
boar who dragged her over
the coals of his hellish wrath
everyday. She swore
he brushed his teeth
with brimstone and swallowed
half of it. He ate her hope
like a dragon did trees.

How she managed to stay
married to someone so vile
amazed half of New Augusta.
The other half prayed he would
be eaten by a panther or
shoot himself by accident
in the deer stand, the closest
he would ever come
to the pearly gates.

Wedding Rings and Chicken Wire Dredging

My babysitter was not the most gracious lady in Perry County often given to bouts of hysteria and hilarity. She could lose her temper, way too easily. But she liked the outdoors and took me and her kids, a menagerie of brutes, to play in the Bogue Homa one afternoon. We laughed and splashed each other until we heard her scream, strong enough to turn the sunlight day into a stormy one filled with threatening tornadoes. She had lost her diamond ring; it had slipped as easily off her finger as the swear words we heard her say and which my mother said were not part of a lady's vocabulary. But my babysitter was in no mood to be polite, and her rough cries caught the attention of two fishermen who rushed toward her to see if she had been bitten by a diamond head or a moccasin. Her fear was worse. Her third wedding ring was lost. Luckily, the men were skilled in the art of chicken wire dredging, and they pulled a roll of it from their sack of stream-side equipment and began pulling it back and forth in the Bogue Homa, up and down, shifting and shifting the wire until the grains of sand that held the ring finally gave it up. The diamond rose to the top of the stream which reminded me of the old woman in the Bible who searched her house, turning it upside down to find a small lost coin. But my babysitter was not a Biblical woman and the two ring diggers were more at home with a pint of Jack or some chew than catching fish which held sacred truths in their mouths.

My Black Spiritual Mother
Beaumont, MS, 1979; in Memory of Caroline "Co" Bolton

On my 40th birthday I thought of Co
holding me in the wooden pew years ago,
an iron-willed, resolute Black woman,
a guardian of tenderness, her calloused hands
assuring me of comfort and security.

There we sat, me a white baby on her
red-aproned lap listening to the preacher
pounding on the pulpit, frightening me
to the point of tears were it not
for Co's nestling me in the love of her arms.

All around us white fans with black faces
behind them; the only comfort churchgoers
had in this late summer heat. So fitting
since the preacher mentioned the word
hell with almost every sentence. I, too,
wanted Co and me to have fans.

I recalled this day in a dream where
Co opened the doors to heaven
with her shepherd-like spirit and
I saw Jesus with her, not the anemic
white Jesus but a dark sinned Galilean
standing right next to Co.

The light was so penetrating in my
dream that it shone through
the windowless country church
where Co once held me. I knew then
she had saved me, one of those
lost babies down in Egypt land.

The Plowman's Tears

Six weeks out from carotid and
triple bypass surgery, Grandpa
slashed his acid tongue at me.

We were in the feed store, his heavy
shoulders rolled from years arguing
with the land as he exploded his plowman's thoughts.

As he ranted, I slipped my purse strap
over my arm, withering as a blue-black,
purple hull in the July sun,
and walked out, in all my 19 years offended, hurt.

Four blocks later, down Richton's Main Street
with only one stop light, usually red,
I relented after an hour and walked
back to the now less fiery, bull of a man waiting,

shaky, his tears meeting and flowing
over mine. His hide-tearing words gone.
After decades, his heavy plow lifted from me.

Calvary Baptist Church
Tucker Bay Church, March 1947

The cement blocks were built
for country white souls
praying away to Jesus

on a Jerusalem dark night
in New Augusta, Mississippi
half a century away from my youth.

A cotton field truck had brought
the blocks out to where the church rose.

It had a two room Sunday school,
one for each gender except
when summer heat dissolved them

on those sultry calico nights
when the church women

fanned themselves to keep
their precious Lord close
and the devil away.

It was then, children rang the bells
for singing and worship
that sounded like courtship invitations.

While the sermons were fiery,
they never quite burned
hot enough to stop the raging boys
eager to invite the girls

to supper on the church's supple grass,
chicken and dumplings and a spread of deserts
on a barbed wire table for these last suppers.

Jesus never tasted so good.

The Baptism at Arlington
Arlington Community, MS, 1986

On a humid Saturday night
the youth leader drove us over
the Leaf River for a church rally
where the light speared its way

through the pines
and where young voices of faith
echoed down the hill
all the way to where the house boats
were bobbing on the river's edge.

We were slowly immersed there
disturbing a congregation of mosquitoes
and the lightning bugs blinked Biblical verses
as if Adam and Eve in Eden were listening.

Serpent in the Red Dirt

The rattle blowing through the
oak trees warning us, landowners
cannot rid themselves
of the influence of this scaly,
blotted, poisonous sliding
through the red dirt, springs,
creeks, over the hills and hollers,
taking forests down in their wake.

We call upon the waters that rim the earth,
flowing into rivers and streams, that fall
upon our gardens and fields.

We fight and the more we fight,
the harder to kill the line stretching,
pumping and pulling every mineral
from beneath this Eden. The death,
destruction and evil, a penetrating
legless essence tricking Eve's sons
and daughters into breaking
the commandment with the land.

We call upon the forests and creatures
of the fields and the seas, our brother
and sisters who share this home.
You brood of vipers!
How will you escape being
condemned to hell? I am sending

you out like sheep among serpents,
yet I have made you to ground
your heel on the head and twist
and stomp to overcome
every one of them.

We call upon all that we hold sacred,
the presence and power
to flow through us.

With the spirit of hope, we will pick
up the bronze serpent
on a staff and hang it high
above these pine trees.
And the land will be cured.

The Meanest Man I Knew

I watched his soaring along the Leaf River sandbar
as he emerged from the moccasin-filled waters, laughing,
the once meanest man burdened with liquor,
roaring among the conifers.

His drinking fists quieted now, he received
a redeeming palm turning pages of Scripture
for the quest of his soul and for others.

A couple weeks ago, and two miles from home,
while standing in the wilderness, I heard a new hymn
springing from my cousin's voice,
the crawling, repulsive man that I knew.

He had fallen to his knees in church, declaring
testimonies from his once harrowing voice,
giving up his fleshly life for the robe of the spirit,
bringing him into a new life of intoxication.

Thirteen Bridges

The clop, clip, clop of the wiper blades
did not clear the block of ice
waiting for her. Rolling across
the thirteen county bridges
to her job at the Pepsi plant.

Time was tired that morning,
her body strained to meet the demands
of the 4:30 alarm o'clock.

Her grey truck blended into
the wintry mix as the clouds
steadily covered the wild beauty of U.S. 98.
But the hungry ditches waited for her.

The sign reading entering Forrest County from
Perry County did not spell her obituary.
Blessedly, she saw the shadow
before the devilish deer could pounce.

She crossed the last bridge
to travel to the plant.
The whistle blew close at hand
as the beeping alarm clock,
Gabriel's horn never sounded so loud.

Graining God in the Morning Hay Field

A low mooing serenades the sun
over a spring morning,
an isolated moment in time hearing God
as mist rises from the grass.

I come here to my sanctuary
before the old DAG tractor roars
to life and the hay baler whines.

At the edge of the straight oak line,
I pitch my tent to look
across the uncut field
in my far-right vision to
the bluegill, bass, and catfish pond.

The grass cut yesterday and raked into lines
to be compressed into the baler
and rolled up, then bound
into a circular mold to preserve.

God has inscribed the spherical imprint on
the surface of this tremulous, golden field,
and on the face of the deep at
the boundary of light and darkness,

Nothing is hidden from the light.

At All the Broken Places

Withered and worn after years
of birthing milk calves, the mother
of herds, she finally succumbed

to gravity and lay dormant in
the autumn-hazed barn,
her eyes asking for deliverance
from the pain of old age.

Too reverent to our life, we could not
send her off to cow burial on
that splintered wooden hearse
and so we banded together,

all six of us to raise her to the dignity
and kindness that she deserved.
We heaved and hauled, a pulley
of love for this old cow raising her

and letting her see the sunlight
that warmed her and her offspring
for so many seasons. But no one
animal or man can be suspended

in air for too long;
the angels might begrudge
of this old cow, and so we
lowered her once more but not

all the way to the barn floor,
just enough to give her hooves
enough space to walk once more.

Spilling Wisdom

Time stopped your last breath,
but your words still speak to me.

Your voice fills the dining room
as we eat our breakfast biscuits
with molasses and cream.
Answers don't come easy anymore.

If I could sit with you now
at that two-sheets of plywood
and four by four table, looking out

the window across the hay field
with you spilling your wisdom
as we sip our coffee, stirring shadows.

Momma is behind us at the stove
cooking the meal that will get us
through the morning. I am like a slick,
newborn calf on a spring day.

The seasons and years have fast-paced
and years later an old mother cow I stand
in the sharp winter wind, staggering
to find my Jordan stream.

Wavering and slowly moaning
your voice calls from the other side,
waiting patiently for the shot to end it all.

What We Cannot See

Nothing works the way
it used to… sprain your hand
in the washer, the shower door breaks.

Collapses on the floor,
and my neighbor steals
the lock off the cattle gate

in the shade of live oaks.
The master lock was my grandfather's
and locked the cows in,

long story short, bored with
his watch marking time,
the country boy needed to make a point
and scratch the dirt like a bull
protecting his herd.

Be wary and wise of a bull
in heat or angry, he can't
see the light in front of him.

All the brightness he could not see
behind the aggravation
of having to open and close
the gate each day to go home.

Tiny stones by the catfish pond
released the days heat,
and the cows low calmly
in the Bahia grass field,

sun sinking out of sight,
waiting for eyes to adjust.

A Smoke-Filled Marriage
New Augusta, MS, 1966

One Sunday in early autumn
the preacher and deacons lined up
all the children at Calvary Church,
herding them up and down the aisles.
He said the Holy Spirit was upon us
like the smoke mists in the trees,
and that we would be baptized
two weeks from today.

As I stepped into Old Mill Creek,
it was cold as a January night and
the preacher's wrinkled, stiff hands plunged
me beneath the smoke colored, cleansing water
and turned me to ash grey.
He said a few words that had no meaning
until I lost the bloom on my face.

Years later, weeding my garden
of briars, brush, and loganberries,
redden my hands by the fire I felt,
I could not get them clean enough.
It was then that the wise preacher's words
about hell came back to me.

I walked out of a painful,
smoke-filled marriage that day.

Cheating

Before all this went down,
Cuck and his friends were playing
Hearts on the front porch for about an hour
or more before Cecille came out
looking like she had been chewing fire.
She heard Cuck's car pull up
and he was not getting out alive.
He broke at least 12 Perry County rules
about courtship and cheating.

He had lived with Cecille down the road
for about seven years and she ferried
herself between a common law husband
and the one whose vows were muttered to.

Cuck had a woman in every curve of Angelhead.
He was drunk at his own wedding
and stayed that way pretty much during the marriage.
Everyone knew about Cecille's dual husbands
but not too many knew who had been sneaking
around with her fifteen-year-old daughter, Boo,
now, pregnant.

She might not have had a sixth grade
education but that day she had a degree
in murder.

Lighting One Post at a Time

The storm barreled up from
the Gulf Coast and then took
a turn and fizzled in Perry County.

Toppling trees and downing
power lines like spaghetti
on these untended, rocky country roads.

Unafraid of what the dark hid,
my wiry uncle manned a chainsaw,
his headlight glowing from his hunter's cap

and joined the Singing River Electric linemen
on the ridge of Kaiser Hill to cut out buried roads,
pointing and telling folks where
to drive in the blacktop full of trees.

By next Sunday afternoon, quiet returned
as a cardinal flew back home.

An Elegy Written at the Old Bethany Graveyard

The dead of New Augusta wear white
tombstones with flags
from the Spanish American War
like those old-fashioned
veterans wore with intricate, scrolling
around their column lapels 150 years ago.

Some were named after
presidents such as Martin Van Buren
Hinton or Grover Cleveland Garner.
They wish they could still vote.

Their names indented so time
or sand or overbearing bushes
did not easily cover them. But they still
showed their business cards
present to any eyes coming by.

I went to school with their great,
great grandsons who rarely
come here to see or talk with
their ancestors beneath their feet.

But souls have a habit
in Perry County of sticking
around long after their bodies
are forgotten.

The Pain that Kept the Grandfather from Dying

The family crossed the Pascagoula River
at dawn, their worry of grief nearly ended
after two years since their grandfather
entered the nursing home.

His sons had longed for him to die
and will them the bottom land
that the vengeful Leaf could not steal.

The anger fuming in their memory of him
sunk below the surface of their veins
drowning his harsh words now.

But they could not escape the pain of
his hard hands and crushing tongue
that always overwhelmed them.

The old man's memory of them
was the memory of the river,
pulling and tugging at him

to go deep black beyond
the sun's bright rays,
where his ancestors waited for him.

They hurt each other so long;
he was in so much pain
that he couldn't die.

Unto Dust

Birth: September 11, 1911—Death: July 30, 1991

Caroline, known as our Co, sits at the doorway,
me at her bowed knees and kind hands,
as an early, spring dusts our cornfields.

An unholy cross once burned in front of her house,
now scattered to ashes. She lived with us,
across from Grandpa, in the middle of the house

with no windows. But she could always see outside
and beyond the horizons of her eyes. She knew
more about the seasons than the *Farmers' Almanac.*

On the back porch, our aunts and cousins
came to visit her as she cooked white-fluffy biscuits.
Our holy communion topped off

with candied figs and hogshead cheese,
a mixture of clear jelly. Her Black
hands sliced it so carefully, almost like a surgeon.

She was our banker, too, hiding money and
family tears in the slits of our boscage walls.
We depended on her nifty, soul-rejoicing safekeeping.

She stewarded our safety, protecting us
from bees, fire ants, rabid dogs rushing
into our yard, and moonshined sharecroppers
looking for easy cash in our house.

She died after heavy years of child rearing, chopping
cotton, and stewing collard greens and turnips
always ready to feed our family country feasts.

When her soul crossed over the muddy
Bogue Homa, my uncles and cousins wanted
to bury her in a separate field far from

the graves of so many of us that she birthed,
buried now under decaying crosses
and behind an old rusty iron fence.

As soon as her body was lowered
into the ground, the dust sung out
as a flock of crows flew over her grave.

Juliet Hinton has been the Cancer Registry Manager in Research and Informatics at Forrest General Hospital for over twenty-two years. Her metaphoric vision of landscape, feminine voice, and the miseries and mercies of Perry County poems published in *Tipton Poetry Journal, Delta Poetry Review, San Pedro Review, Cantos, Valley Voices Literary Review*, and other literary journals. In January 2022, she received Pushcart Prize Nomination for"Calvary Baptist Church" published in *Delta Poetry Review*. She is currently working on more Perry County and landscape poems, and a new project on oncology cancer care. Additionally, she has been nominated for Poet Laureate of Perry County.

www.ingramcontent.com/pod-product-compliance
Lightning Source LLC
Chambersburg PA
CBHW022054080426
42734CB00009B/1337